I Am More Than My Experiences

Workbook

A Woman's Transformational Journey
To Discovering Her True Identity

Allen and Lloyda Forbes

Published by Allen Forbes
P.O. Box 305
Germantown, MD 20875

Cover design by Alloy Consulting Group LLC
Cover photo by Alexandr Ivanov (used with permission)

Your experiences do not have to define who you are!

Table of Contents

Module One:
The Repeat

Points to ponder

A. Identity consists of three things: belief system, personality, and DNA.

B. Identity is an internal conviction that leads to a behavior, which affirms existence.

C. Understanding your identity is crucial if you desire to advance and be your most authentic self.

D. Experiences, environments, individuals, and groups can help form identity.

E. Identity is tied to purpose.

What parts of your past do you seem to repeat? Be specific about the areas or instances.

_____

_____

_____

_____

_____

_____

_____

_____

Why do you believe that you are in a repeating cycle in these areas of your life?

_____

_____

_____

_____

_____

_____

_____

_____

_____

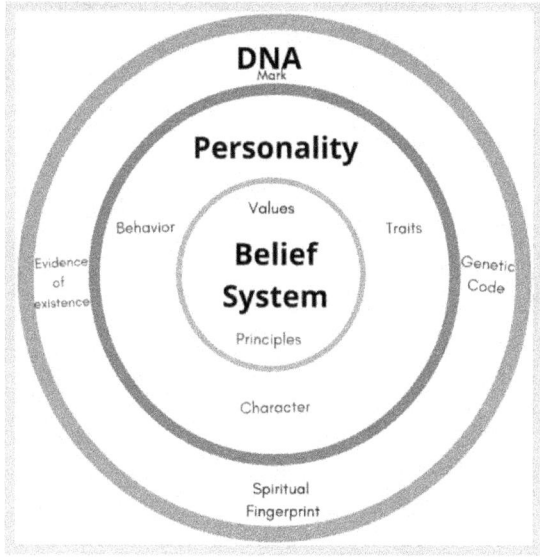

Knowing that your belief system is a part of your identity, what would you say are your core beliefs?

_____

_____

_____

_____

Where do you think your beliefs have come from? (Experiences, people or other influences)

_____

_____

_____

Social Group Blending Process

Taste

Touch

Association & Experience

Feeling, Thinking & Image

Group Identity

Look & Sight

Behavior

Talk & Sound

Seeing

Hearing

Smell

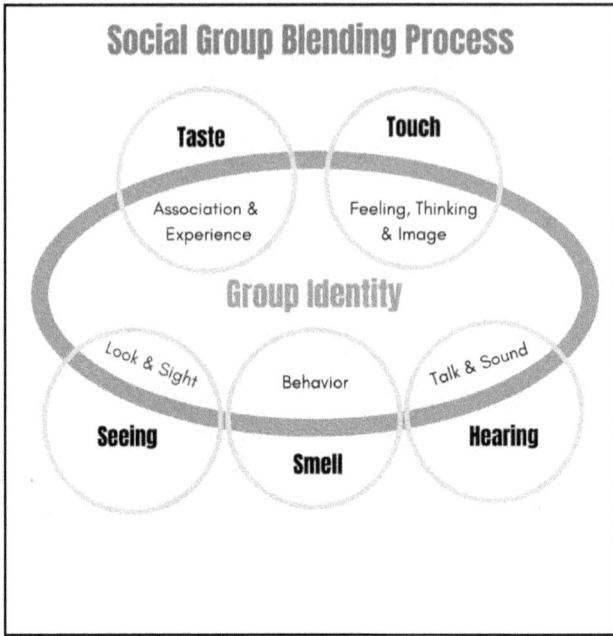

The social group blending process causes you to look, feel, act, smell, sound and taste like the group that has accepted you.

What has your social group blending process been like?

_____

_____

_____

_____

_____

_____

_____

1. List four individuals that were a part of your social group blending process. Underneath their names, write the positive and negative outcomes of that blending process.

Individual #1: _____

Positives: _____

_____

_____

Negatives: _____

_____

_____

Individual #2: _____

Positives: _____

_____

_____

Negatives: _____

_____

_____

Individual #3: _____

Positives: _____

_____

_____

Negatives: _____

_____

_____

Individual #4: _____

Positives: _____

_____

_____

Negatives: _____

_____

_____

2. Take the positive attributes from these individuals and create a list of positive attributes that you need to be around. Do the same with the negative attributes (add some attributes that you know you should avoid.)

This will show you what you should look for in individuals that you socialize with going forward and will also help you discover your "social group dream team."

_____

_____

_____

_____

_____

_____

_____

Because your behavior is based on your identity, what does your behavior tell you about how you view your identity? Additionally – ask those closest to you what your behavior tells them about your identity.

_____

_____

_____

_____

_____

_____

_____

When you are behaving in a way that disturbs others or yourself, try to capture what you are feeling and thinking about. Write your responses below. Clue - you may feel anger or shame, but dig in deeper and find out what is really at the root of those emotions.

_____

_____

_____

_____

_____

Note: Getting to the root is the way to start the process of making significant behavior change.

If identity is your personal mark that leaves evidence that you were present, what do you believe is the purpose of the mark that you are supposed to leave?

_____

_____

_____

_____

_____

_____

_____

_____

_____

_____

_____

_____ -

_____

_____

Module Two:
The Exchange

Points to ponder

A. What is the Lord requesting from me?

B. What do I have that I can give/surrender to God?

C. During my prayer time do I give the Lord time to also share with me?

Sometimes, going through unpleasant or traumatic experiences can derail you from your destination, or from being the person you were created to be. What are some of the things that you believe have altered your "trip setting"?

_____

_____

_____

_____

_____

One of my wife's friends shared with me recently that she was hitting a ceiling, spiritually. She said that her interpretation of what God was saying was being filtered by her past experiences. This obviously caused her deep frustration. After a few moments of silence, she took a deep breath and her next statement described the reason for her feeling this way: "I feel like I need to replace my dirty filter."

a) What is it about your "filter" that needs to be replaced, in order to see your future as God sees it?
b) How is your 'filter' affecting the way that you view your experiences?

_____

_____

_____

_____

We usually come to God with our requests and that is the extent of our prayer. However, consider the fact that God wants to have a conversation with us and there is an exchange; we give to Him and He gives to us.

Jesus started a conversation with her (woman at the well) and said, "Give me a drink." John 4:7

Are you surprised to know that you have something to offer God? Do you see yourself as someone with something to offer?

If not, why?

_____

_____

If yes, what?

_____

_____

How can you use what you have to serve God and humanity?

_____

_____

_____

_____

_____

It was at this well where Jesus had a conversation with a woman, who, according to Pharisee practice, was not worthy of His words. At a time when Jesus should not have been talking to this woman at the well, He decided to have a verbal exchange with her. She was coming to the well to get water and have her thirst quenched. *She was driven to the well (a place of provision) by a need. In that place, she gave to Jesus and He gave to her.*

What are some of the needs and wants that have driven you? Where have they driven you?

_____

_____

_____

_____

_____

_____

_____

Module Three:
Identify

<u>Points to ponder</u>

A. Have I been seeking natural things first?

B. What has my thirst caused me to pursue?

C. How do I get from a wilderness mentality to a Promised Land mentality?

Identifying Your Thirst

There is a natural thirst and a spiritual thirst.

The definition of thirst is a strong desire or longing that is, or seems of necessity. A need can be real, or imagined. It could seem like a need. You have to determine whether it's really a need, or if it's something that just appears to be a need. We can become so impulse-driven that we act from a place of perceived need, rather than actual need.

What are you "thirsty" for? Is it real?

_____

_____

_____

Will it benefit you in the long run or will it bring more hurt than peace?

_____

_____

_____

Matthew 5:6 says, *"Blessed are they which do hunger and thirst after righteousness: for they shall be filled."* There must be an understanding of thirst: what it is,

where it comes from, and how it can be addressed so that it does not create a spiritual 'disconnect.'
Thirst causes pursuit.

What has your thirst caused you to pursue?

_____

_____

_____

_____

A lack of thirst, or a thirst for unhealthy things can cause a failure to thrive.

When you pursue spiritual things, you are alive. However, when you pursue people or things that don't add to you positively, it creates a form of death, which is a failure to thrive.

Has there been a person or thing that has created a failure to thrive mentality in your life?

_____

_____

_____

_____

_____

_____

What we do naturally is not going to quench the thirst for what we need spiritually. Spiritual needs have to be addressed through spiritual means.

Thirst builds passion.

When passion is directed in the right way, it will link you to your purpose.

What things can you do to allow your spiritual thirst to fuel your passion toward unlocking your purpose?

_____

_____

_____

_____

Spiritual Needs Cycle

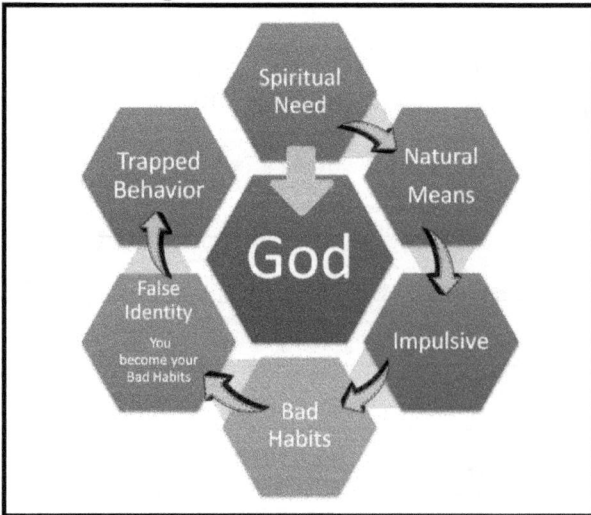

In what ways can you prioritize God first in your life?

_____

_____

_____

_____

_____

_____

_____

_____

_____

_____

_____

_____

_____

_____

_____

_____

_____

_____

Module Four:
Inquest

Points to ponder

A. What are your dreams?

B. When your eyes are closed what do you see? Be honest.

C. What do you want to see (when your eyes are closed?)

D. Are you defined by your experiences or by what God says about you?

The woman at the well had to do some introspection. This meeting with Jesus caused questions to arise within her. She did not realize that the questions at the well would lead to the same questions she would later have to ask herself. While the questions started off from a natural perspective, they would later expand into spiritual questions. I call these "the well questions."

"Well" Questions

"Why" has to do with your purpose.
Why am I here?

_____

_____

_____

What is your reason for existing?

_____

_____

_____

What are you good at?

_____

_____

_____

_____

What do you enjoy doing?

_____

_____

_____

_____

_____

_____

What do you hate? What causes you strong emotion?

_____

_____

_____

_____

_____

"What and how"

How are you going to accomplish your purpose?

_____

_____

_____

_____

_____

What are the natural and sequential ordered steps that you can take towards completing your goal?

_____

_____

_____

Create an action plan. What are the first steps?

_____

_____

_____

_____

_____

_____

_____

_____

_____

_____

Where?

Determine the resources needed. Don't worry about where they are going to come from. When God gives the vision, He will give the provision.

What resources (natural and spiritual) do you need?

_____

_____

_____

_____

_____

_____

_____

Where also determines your destination. Where is your end result?

_____

_____

_____

_____

_____

_____

_____

Who?

Who are you? The Creator of all things knows your purpose. Ask the Creator, God "Who am I?" Your identity comes from Him.

Who are you? Not what do you do, but who are you?

_____

_____

_____

_____

_____

_____

What makes you unique?

_____

_____

_____

_____

_____

_____

How can you use your uniqueness and differences to affect change in your environment?

_____

_____

_____

_____

_____

_____

_____

_____

People have defined us by our own actions, their actions, and what we have permitted or allowed to take place in our lives.

In what ways have you allowed others to define you?

_____

_____

_____

_____

_____

_____

_____

_____

_____

_____

_____

_____

Module Five:
Attachment

<u>**Points to ponder**</u>

A. Are there things that you have an attachment to?

B. Why do you think you have this attachment?

C. What do you fear about letting this attachment go?

Everything you do has a corresponding action. In Physics, Newton says that whenever you push against something, there is a force pushing back at you, which is called "resistance". If I push my son's toy car across the kitchen floor, it pushes back with a force. I don't feel it because I am applying more force than the toy car has. On the other hand, when I go outside and try to push my car, I can immediately feel the car pushing back at me with force. When I use a greater force than the car, the car will move. Spiritual force is the same. For progress to be made spiritually, we need to use a greater force than our opposition. God is power and there is nothing greater than His force.

In Mark 5:25-29, a woman had an issue, and she spent all that she had. She was literally and figuratively spent! When we have an issue, we spend time, money, and resources to figure a way out. This happens often. We start running around and doing a lot of natural things and lose our focus. Many times, we hide our issues from everyone. We may even try to hide it from God, but He knows, so there is no sense in being false. Bring it to Him, to the One who can liberate you. Be open honest with Him and with yourself.

What has been your biggest challenge?

_____

_____

_____

_____

What type of thoughts and emotions do you have concerning your challenge?

_____

_____

_____

_____

Are you hiding any issues from God? If so, why?

_____

_____

_____

_____

_____

Do you make excuses or blame others for your issue? Are you content with living with it?

_____

_____

_____

_____

_____

_____

Is there something about this issue that you like, e.g., does it make you feel good, or comfortable? Does it bring you security and pleasure? Be honest.

_____

_____

_____

_____

_____

_____

_____

_____

_____

_____

_____

_____

_____

_____

_____

_____

Module Six:
Un-Wrap

Grace: The force that delivers

<u>Points to Ponder</u>

A. Can you identify any self-defeating habits in your life?

B. Un-wrapping your association with the issue wraps you in God's grace.

C. What/whom do you look for to feel secure?

D. What is your environment like and what do you need to change about it?

E. Self-reflection is needed to have the right perception and to have the right perspective.

When we take our issues to our Creator, He exchanges our issues and gives us a touch, an encounter that wraps us in His grace. *When we un-wrap our association with the issue, He wraps us in grace!!* Then, what we could not do in our natural strength becomes easier with His grace. His grace is not just unmerited favor, but His power, force, and ability actually work through us.

What natural practices or habits do you need to stop?

_____

_____

_____

_____

_____

_____

In what ways can you make Jesus the priority in your life? What will that look like?

_____

_____

_____

_____

_____

_____

The right perception of yourself clears the way for you to have the right perspective

Knowing that you are a Daughter of God, write down how you should see yourself? How should you feel?

_____

_____

_____

_____

_____

_____

What will you no longer tolerate in your life?

_____

_____

_____

_____

With no obstacles in your way, what is the first thing you will do?

_____

_____

_____

Affirmation

Making an affirmation of what you want to have in your life is a good starting point. As you begin this journey of developing your best self, speaking positive words over yourself and into your atmosphere will help create an environment for advancement and accomplishment. Below is an affirmation that you can use each day to help you feel empowered and charged. Remember it is God's grace that empowers us! Say this:

Lord, You are bigger and larger than any issue that I am facing. Today, I partake of Your grace and I will not thirst after the wrong things. *I am spiritually sound and I am more than my experiences!*

The Lord's light has healed me of past hurts and emotional pain. I am emotionally, physically and spiritually balanced and healthy. All generational curses are broken in my life and the generational blessings will proceed forward with me and the generations after me. I speak victory over every issue that I have fought with and struggled with. Today I will experience a touch from the Lord. With His grace and empowerment I have the power to conquer what has tried to conquer me. The anointing is released now over my life. I have been set free. I am led by the Lord. I know what to do spiritually and naturally and I will not fall into the trap of the enemy. Today, I am free!

I am a daughter/son of the King. I am surrounded with people who love me, see me, and care for me. Evil, jealous and harmful people are removed from my path.

My steps are ordered by the Lord. The Lord illuminates me with His light and my true identity is exposed. I am courageous, strong, bold, and secure. I am focused, confident, powerful and fearless. I am "more than!"

Today I see myself, I will be myself and I will agree with myself.

If you enjoyed this workbook, please leave a favorable review on www.Amazon.com

Introduction to the King

Maybe by some off-chance you picked up this book and you have never met the King. I would like to take this time to introduce you to Him. He came, bled and died for you because He loves you. His name is Jesus and He longs to have a relationship with you. In order to have this relationship with Him you will have to invite Him to come and live in your heart. You can do this by praying and inviting Him in. If you would like to do so, please read the prayer below and then pray it to Him with sincerity.

Prayer
God -- I am a sinner and I believe that Jesus died for the forgiveness, atonement and remission of my spiritual and natural sin. You loved me so much that you gave your Son so I could be a part of your family. I believe that Jesus Christ was raised from the dead and is my Lord and Savior. Jesus, I invite You to come and live in my heart. Please lead and guide me as my new Lord in the kingdom of God.

It is that simple (Romans 10:9). If you prayed and believe this prayer, please reach out to us so that we can connect with you. It is vital that you find a good bible believing church that you can become a part of. Continue to read the bible to discover your true identity. Be who God has said that you are.

Welcome to the Kingdom! Enjoy getting to know the King of Kings.

About the Author

Allen Forbes is a Christian author and speaker who is dedicated to encouraging others to recognize and pursue their identity in God. He is a licensed minister, with a background of 20+ years of faithful serving and stewardship in ministry. Allen has spent decades in the business arena in roles that included service, management, sales, and entrepreneurship. He is the co-founder of Living Life International -- a faith-based nonprofit that inspires, educates and informs. You will find a combination of biblical principles, humor and extensive business wisdom in his books and presentations. Originally from Brooklyn, NY Allen and his family reside in Maryland.

Connect with Allen through social media

www.facebook.com/AuthoringInspiration

www.instagram.com/allen.forbes.12

About the Author

Minister Lloyda Forbes ("ML") is a teacher of the Gospel, a worshipper and intercessor, who has served in lay ministry for more than a decade. She also leads the **H.I.S.** Daughter women's ministry – which empowers women in rising to their kingdom identity. She is a part of the ministerial staff of **VCCI**, and has faithfully served the vision in various positions of leadership for more than 20 years.

Lloyda Forbes holds a degree in Organizational Management, and various certifications in mental/social-emotional health, by which she provides sensitive and informed care to the community-at-large. An evolving learner, Lloyda has enjoyed a varied tenure in the marketplace; with ownership in the for-profit, as well as nonprofit sector, as a coach, facilitator, administrative professional, and workforce development trainer. She and her family reside in Maryland.

www.instagram.com/h.i.s.daughter

Other Books

Sandbox Personalities Book

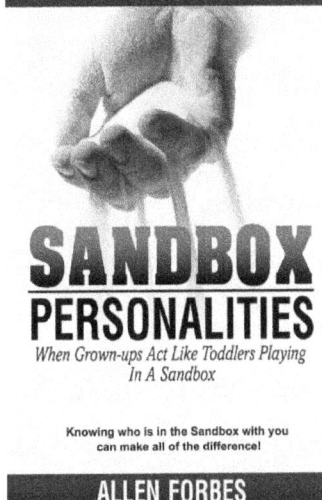

SANDBOX PERSONALITIES

When Grown-ups Act Like Toddlers Playing In A Sandbox

Knowing who is in the Sandbox with you can make all of the difference!

ALLEN FORBES

I Am More Than My Experiences

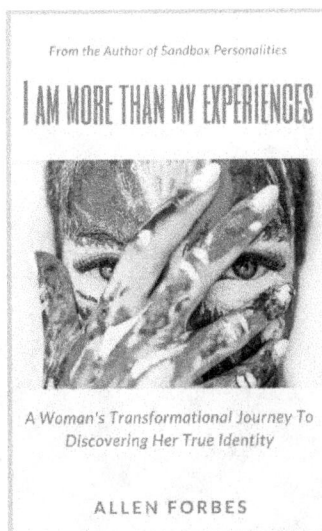

From the Author of Sandbox Personalities

I AM MORE THAN MY EXPERIENCES

A Woman's Transformational Journey To Discovering Her True Identity

ALLEN FORBES

Other Books continued

www.AFspeaks.com

I Am More Than My Experiences Workbook

I AM MORE THAN MY EXPERIENCES

A WOMAN'S TRANSFORMATIONAL JOURNEY TO
DISCOVERING HER TRUE IDENTITY

WORKBOOK

ENVISION A CLEARER PICTURE OF YOU

ALLEN AND LLOYDA FORBES

Kingdom Dynamics

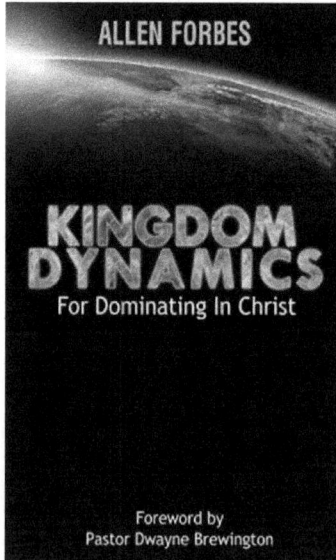

ALLEN FORBES

KINGDOM
DYNAMICS
For Dominating In Christ

Foreword by
Pastor Dwayne Brewington

42

Other Books <small>continued</small>

Dear Daughter Love Dad

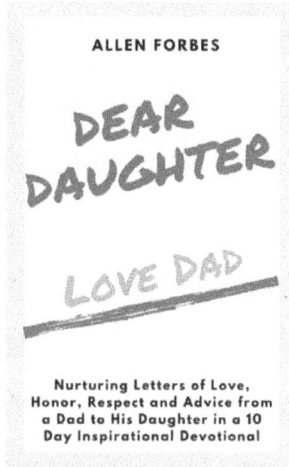

ALLEN FORBES

DEAR
DAUGHTER

LOVE DAD

Nurturing Letters of Love,
Honor, Respect and Advice from
a Dad to His Daughter in a 10
Day Inspirational Devotional

Recommended Audio Resource

Mindful Parenting Live Training

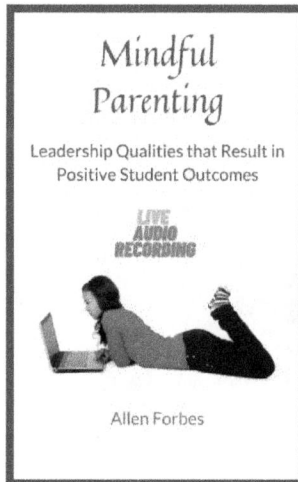

Mindful
Parenting

Leadership Qualities that Result in
Positive Student Outcomes

LIVE
AUDIO
RECORDING

Allen Forbes

www.ingramcontent.com/pod-product-compliance
Lightning Source LLC
Chambersburg PA
CBHW070802050426
42452CB00012B/2465